# Cooking
## for Campers & Backpackers

Victoria and Frank Logue

**Illustrations by Leigh Ellis**

Menasha Ridge Press
Birmingham, Alabama

Printed in the United States of America
Published by Menasha Ridge Press
First edition, first printing


Illustrations  by Leigh Ellis
Text design by Carolina Graphics Group

Menasha Ridge Press
3169 Cahaba Heights Road
Birmingham, Alabama 35243

# Contents

# Introduction

There's no way around it. You're awake. Lying in your tent in the murky light of the getting-ready-for-dawn sky, you know you ought to get moving. Sore from a rough night's sleep, you crawl out of your sleeping bag, wondering why you're in a tent in the woods instead of at home in your bed. You throw on some clothes, climb out of the tent, and fire up the stove. In 15 minutes a cup of coffee has revived your senses and your noises have roused your hiking partner out of her sleeping bag. Together you dice a potato and onion and put them into a skillet with a little oil. By the time the sun bathes the clearing in orange light a few minutes later, you are kicked back enjoying trail eggs (page 14). Suddenly the reason you had to get out on the trail this weekend is clear. It would be hard to explain back at work on Monday, but you know you'll want to be in the woods again soon.

Let's face it. The sunrise didn't hurt, but a little **A little cuisine goes a long way in the backcountry.** cuisine goes a long way in the backcountry. There is nothing like a hearty meal to get you ready for another day in camp or on the trail.

At home you may cook from dozens of different recipes during the year. On the trail, a few good meals can keep you going on years of backpacking. For a weekend trip, you only need two breakfasts, two lunches and a dinner and those meals must be simple to prepare, or you won't want to make them in camp. Backcountry cooking is almost always done on a single burner stove with a limited fuel supply. This book gives 25 recipes and lots of other suggestions. Most of the recipes are one-pot meals that take no more than 20 minutes to cook. Unless otherwise noted, the recipes are intended for two.

Bon Apetit!

# Stoves

Camping and backpacking have become more earth friendly activities in the past ten years. Almost all campers cook on a stove instead of a fire. It's not that fires are all bad, but denuding the woods to feed the fire goes against the grain of environmentally sound camping. In some parks and forests, fires are prohibited, and during times of low rainfall, areas normally open to campfires won't allow them. So it is not a question of whether you need a camp stove, but which stove you want.

## Selecting a Stove

To decide which stove to buy, you must know how you want to use it. If you are going to be car camping, a two-burner white gas or propane stove is a good choice. If you are going to be doing some backpacking, you will want a lightweight backpacking stove. If foreign travel is in your plans, you will need a multi-fuel stove, and if mountaineering is in your future, you will need a high output stove.

> **To decide which stove to buy, you must know how you want to use it.**

The fuel a stove uses is an important factor in your selection. In the United States, the most popular stoves burn white gas. They must be primed and can be finicky at times, but with a little experience, lighting and using a white gas stove becomes second nature.

Kerosene and alcohol stoves are popular in Europe. Kerosene stoves need to be primed, but are more tolerant of cold than white gas stoves that must be insulated. Alcohol stoves don't burn as hot as other stoves, but they are inexpensive and don't require priming.

Butane and propane stoves are the easiest to operate. They work like a natural gas stove at home. Butane cartridges must be kept above freezing, and neither propane nor butane can be shipped on an airplane. Multifuel stoves accept at least two types of fuel and often many more. They are expensive, but highly adaptable.

# Using a Camp Stove

These few hard-learned lessons will help you get along with your camp stove:

- Always test cook on a camp stove before you take it into the backcountry. Don't just try firing it up, but actually use it to cook and clean up a complete meal. Read and follow the manufacturer's advice on using your stove.
- Never cook in your tent. No matter how cold or wet you are, cook outside of the tent or in the vestibule.
- Cook on a flat, stable, non-flammable surface.
- Carry a repair kit for your stove. They are lightweight, take up very little space, and are invaluable if your stove sputters to a halt when you're getting hypothermic.
- Slip foam beverage container around a butane cartridge to keep it warm.
- Use the manufacturers heat deflector or windscreen to reduce fuel consumption. Make sure that the pot doesn't fill up the area of the windscreen or too much heat will build up under your stove (an explosive situation).
- Never refill your stove near a fire or other flame or if the stove is hot.
- When refilling your gas fuel bottle or stove, only fill it three-fourths full to allow room for pressure to build.
- Pre-filter any low-grade fuel you use to avoid clogs and repairs later. Most manufacturers offer filters for their gas stoves.

- When putting away your gear after a trip, always clean your stove. Unless you use a propane or butane stove, empty the fuel as well.
- Test fire your stove before you take it into the backcountry, if you haven't used it in more than a couple of months.
- Liquid fuels have a short shelf life. Replace your fuel if it is more than a year old.

# Cooking Pots and Utensils

Most of your backcountry meals will be cooked in one pot or pan, so you don't have to burden yourself with a lot of unnecessary gear. One two-quart pot with a lid, two drinking cups, two bowls, two spoons and two pocket knives are all that you and your companion will need. An eight-inch frying pan and a spatula will add versatility to your cookware, and you can also carry a frisbee as your food plate. It allows for generous servings and you can play with it between meals. By using a plastic or metal measuring cup as your drinking cup, you get double duty out of your mug.

**Most of your backcountry meals will be cooked in one pot or pan.**

A little more communal equipment is needed for four or more hikers. A four-quart pot with a lid, ten-inch frying pan, mixing bowl, and big wooden spoon (it's light and doesn't heat up when stirring) are essential for group cooking. A grater, measuring cup, and pot holders are optional items you may want to consider. How much gear you carry will depend on whether you are carrying it 10 feet from the car or 20 miles into the backcountry.

# Water

"It looks good to me."

That's about all you or your camping buddies can say when checking out a campsite's water source. Even in cool weather without a lot of exertion, you'll need at least two liters of water per person per day, so a good source of water quickly becomes important. If the water source is not a tap from a public water supply, it must be considered suspect and hence, treated. Boiling, chemical treatment, and water filters are the preferred methods of making even beaver pond water safe to drink.

## Boiling

Water used in most recipes is treated while you cook. Bringing the water to a boil kills off parasites, such as *Giardia lamblia* and viruses, including hepatitis. There is some debate concerning how long to boil water before it is safe. Some doctors say that simply bringing water to a boil is enough to kill any contaminants, while others counter that you must boil the water for five minutes. Either way, water used in meals or for hot drinks can be easily treated by boiling.

The main drawback to treating water by boiling it is that it must cool down before you can drink it alone or in drink mixes, such as Kool-aid.

**Water used in meals or for hot drinks can be easily treated by boiling.**

## Chemical Treatment

Iodine tablets are the surest method of chemical treatment. The drawbacks are that it takes about 20 minutes to treat the water and leaves a bad aftertaste. When backpacking though, it is easy to put purification tablets into the water as you fill your canteens. By the time you get thirsty, the water will be purified.

Some campers use a few drops of chlorine to treat their water. Water treatment experts at the Centers for Disease Control say that this is an unsafe method. Water purity, temperature, and a host of other factors go into determining how much chlorine is needed. It is too complicated to calculate a safe treatment using chlorine in the field.

**It is too complicated to calculate a safe treatment using chlorine in the field.**

# Filtering

Water filters have become increasingly common in the backcountry as campers have become more aware of Giardia and other water-borne parasites. Water filters range in price from $40-$150. Most water filters remove bacteria, but leave viruses untreated. While this is not generally a problem in the United States, hepatitis, typhus, and other viruses pose a serious threat to international travellers. Some filters also chemically treat as they filter to remove all impurities.

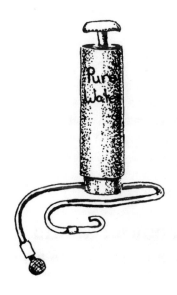

# Food

## Nutrition

There are stories of Civilian Conservation Corps workers in the 1930's venturing off on an overnight trip without anything but the clothes on their backs and a few items in their pockets. They would spend the night under the stars and not even bother to eat for the overnight trip. After all, they only missed two or three meals. That depression-era attitude is long gone, but it's interesting to think what such an unfettered overnight hike would be like.

On an overnight trip, the food you eat doesn't matter all that much, if you are eating a balanced diet at home. But, the longer you will be backpacking or camping, the more important your camp food becomes.

**Carbo loading will help give you fuel to burn while you hike.**

Carbo loading will help give you fuel to burn while you hike. Simple carbohydrates like sugar and honey, and complex carbohydrates like oatmeal, pasta, and rice should be 60-70 percent of your camp diet. The carbohydrates break down easily into the glucose your body needs for energy.

The remainder of the food you eat should be split between proteins and fats. The proteins become the amino acids that keep the body going. Good sources of protein include tuna and other fish, lean meat, beans, and nuts. Fat provides a storehouse of energy. Foods high in fat include salami, cheese, and butter. Your fat intake should be less than 50 grams per day.

## Pre-cooked Meals

The easiest boil-and-eat foods to prepare are the pre-cooked packaged meals that come complete in a foil pouch. Heavy and expensive, they are also the best tasting meals packaged for backpacking. To prepare, drop the pouch in boiling water for five minutes, open, and eat. In a pinch, you can even eat the meals straight from the pouch.

# Drying Your Own Food

If you want to add meat, fruit, or vegetables to your camping meals, drying your own foods is a good way to lighten your pack without sacrificing quality. You can dry food using a conventional oven, but the results are uneven and often dissapointing. The only way to get consistent results is by purchasing a food dryer. The dryers dehydrate food by using heated air to remove up to 95 percent of the moisture.

The drawback to dehydrating food yourself is that it is a time consuming, and often labor-intensive project. It is too daunting a task to prepare all of the food you will need in a dehydrator, but it is easy enough to make enough to supplement your supermarket or freeze-dried diners. At about $80 for a good dehydrator, you will want to plan to dry a lot of food to make it pay off.

# Freeze-Dried Food

The lightest meals are the pre-packaged freeze-dried food available at backpacking stores. With nearly all of their water removed, these meals offer a featherweight alternative for backpackers. They cook up quickly and, with a few added spices, can be quite tasty, although more expensive than supermarket food. You can have the best of both worlds by adding freeze-dried vegetables into your meals. For example, add dried mixed vegetables to tried and true macaroni and cheese for added nutrional value and better taste.

**Freeze-dried meals offer a featherweight alternative for backpackers.**

Popular brands of freeze-dried foods include Alpine Aire, Backpacker's Pantry, Harvest Foodworks, Mountain House, and Richmoor. Practically any food is found in a freeze-dried version, including meat, vegetables, fruit, eggs, and even ice cream. One-, two- and four-person meals are available in a variety that includes dishes such as chicken fajitas, mandarin orange chicken, beef burgundy, or shrimp Cantonese. Most of the companies offer vegetarian meals as well. Freeze-dried meals are good to stash in your pack as an emergency meal. You won't notice the extra weight of a meal in your pack, but you'll appreciate the needed food if you have to spend an unexpected night in the backcountry.

# Supermarket Food

All the food you need for camping and backpacking is as close as the nearest supermarket. Freeze-dried and dehydrated foods are light, but your grocery store has a vast selection of inexpensive alternatives. We have backpacked for thousands of miles without the benefit of pre-packaged backpacking meals. It's not that we never eat freeze-dried or dehydrated food in the backcountry, but don't feel that you must them for an enjoyable trip.

**Your grocery store has a vast selection of inexpensive alternatives.**

The supermarket supplies a ready supply of pasta, rice, and grains, along with fresh eggs, vegetables, and meats. Most food from the grocery store is much less expensive than the freeze-dried or pre-cooked packages and easier than dehydrating your own food. The drawback to supermarket food is that it is the heaviest option. While this isn't a problem if you're car camping, it can be a factor on long distance hikes.

# Breakfast

At home, breakfast is important, but when camping, it is essential. You'll be burning extra calories on a camping or backpacking trip, so the first meal of the day has to give your body plenty of fuel.

**Suggested Breakfasts**
Oatmeal (instant in a variety of flavors)
Cold cereal with powdered milk
Toaster pastries (cold)
Instant grits (a southern favorite)
Creamed Wheat
Eggs (will keep for several days)
Bagels with cream cheese (Cheese will keep for several days.)
Snickers or other candy bars
Breakfast Bars
Granola Bars
Gorp in powdered milk
Pancakes (Bring the dry mix, add powdered milk and water.)
Granola in powdered milk
Instant hash browns
Bacon bars
Canned bacon
Bread with peanut butter
English muffins
Raisin bread

# Breakfast Recipes

### Breakfast Pitas
2 pita pockets                     Cheddar or other hard cheese
One can Spam

Cut the pitas in half and pull the pocket open. Slice the cheese into thin pieces and put 3-4 slices into each pocket half. Open the Spam, cut into 1/4 inch slices, and fry in a frying pan or the bottom of a pot. When the Spam is cooked, slide it into the pita pocket with the cheese. Briefly fry the pita in the same pan to soften the cheese. Canadian bacon or other meat can be substituted for the Spam.

### Trail Eggs
4 eggs                            Cheddar or other hard cheese
1 large potato                    1 small onion and/or green pepper
1 tablespoon oil

*Before you go:* Bring a pot of water to a boil and immerse the eggs for five seconds each. This will seal them and they will keep for a couple of weeks without spoiling. Just be careful to pack them so they don't break. To speed up the cooking process on the trail, bake the potatoes at home for half an hour in the oven (2 1/2 minutes each in the microwave). You can finish cooking them in camp.

*In camp:* Chop potato, onion, and/or green pepper into small pieces. Break open the eggs and beat in a bowl. Cut the cheese into thin very slices. Five or six slices should be about right, but you can add it to taste. Heat the oil in a frying pan or the bottom of a cook pot and toss in the chopped vegetables, stirring continuously, until the onions are translucent. Put the beaten eggs and cheese slices into the pan and stir with a spatula until the eggs are cooked. A spicier version of these trail eggs can be made by using monterey jack cheese with jalepeno peppers.

## Pancakes

| | |
|---|---|
| 1 cup Bisquick | 1/6 cup powdered milk or 1/2 cup milk |
| 1 egg | 1/2 cup fresh or dried fruit such as apples, |
| Margarine or oil | peaches, blueberries, or raspberries |

*At home:* If you are using a real egg, prepare it as descirbed in the previous recipe. If using powdered milk, mix measured amounts of Bisquick and powdered milk together in a resealable bag with a tablespoon of non-dairy creamer.

*In camp:* If you are using dried fruit, rehydrate it first by putting it in a pan, covering it in water and bringing to a low boil. Set off the stove, let cool a couple of minutes and drain.

Mix Bisquick (or combined Bisquick/powdered milk mixture) with milk or water. Add the milk (or water) slowly and stir until you have a well-blended, slightly soupy mixture. Add the fruit and mix well.

Pour pancake mixture into a lightly greased pan leaving room around the sides of the pan. This will allow space to get the spatula in to flip the pancakes. Don't try to do it all at once; one pancake at a time is enough work. As the top of the pancake begins to bubble, flip and cook an equal amount on the opposite side. Serve with syrup, brown sugar, or margarine. Finely chopped walnuts or pecans can be used in place of fruit for a protein-packed variation.

# Lunch

A midday meal is always the hardest to plan for when camping or backpacking. You usually don't want to take the time to make a complicated meal that requires a lot of cleaning up. Many campers opt for a no-cook lunch.

### Suggested Lunches

Summer sausage or pepperoni
Cheese (especially gouda and other wax-wrapped cheeses)
Crackers
Hard-boiled eggs
Fresh vegetables (carrot slices, etc.)
Fresh or dried fruit
Beef Jerky
Sunflower or other seeds
Cookies
Snack cakes
Instant pudding
Gorp (recipe in snack section)
Peanut butter or cheese sandwiches
Sardines
Nuts
Dried soups
Candy bars
Lipton Noodles and Sauce
English muffins and peanut butter
Crackers and tuna
Corned beef or Spam
Granola bars
Pitas stuffed with cheese, etc.
Vienna sausages
Fruit cake

# Lunch Recipes

### Northwoods Bread

1 cup sugar
1/4 cup light Karo syrup
1/2 cup shredded coconut

1 cup margarine
4 1/2 cups rolled oats
1/2 cup chocolate chips

*At home:* This is a make-at-home recipe. Preheat the oven to 350 degrees. Cream the margarine and sugar together. Then add the other ingredients together in a bowl and mix until well blended. Spread on a greased baking sheet to a thickness of one half inch or less. Bake 15-20 minutes or until light brown. Let cool, cut in half so each hiker can have a ready supply for lunch. This also makes a nutritious trailside snack. For variety, add chopped nuts, raisins, or M&Ms in place of or in addition to coconut or chocolate chips.

### Tuna Pitas

2 pita pockets
1 6-ounce can tuna in oil
1/4 teaspoon garlic powder

Gouda, cheddar, or other cheese
1 small can chopped black olives

Cut the pita pockets in half. Drain the can of black olives well away from the trail or camp. Cut the cheese into quarter-inch square chunks. Mix tuna with oil, chunks of cheese, chopped black olives, and garlic powder and spoon into pita pockets.

### Hiker's Loaf

2 six-inch rolls (French or Italian bread)
2 tins sardines packed in oil
1/2 cup green onions (chopped)
Small jar marinated artichoke hearts

1/2 cup radishes, shredded
2 tablespoons olive oil
2 tablespoons white wine vinegar
2 cucumber spears, 6 inches long

*At home:* Cut the rolls in half, horizontally; scoop out most of the insides leaving bread about one-half inch thick. In a bowl, mix sardines, onions, drained and chopped artichoke hearts, radishes, oil, and vinegar. Pack ingredients separately. This meal should be eaten within a few hours of being packed and is intended for the first lunch of your trip.

*In camp:* Fill one half of each roll with mixed ingerdients, and lay a cucumber spear on the other half.

# Dinner

By dinnertime, you'll be tired and hungry. You won't want to spend a lot of time preparing supper, but you'll be in the mood for something good. Now is the time to work a one pot wonder or two. Most of your dinner options start with boiling water. Pasta and rice are the mainstays of camp food, and in 10 minutes (or less) cooking time will provide bulk for your meals. With a little creativity, you can add variety.

**Most of your dinner options start with boiling water.**

Any of these suggested dinners can be prepared with canned or dried meat and some added freeze-dried or dehydrated vegetables. The key is to keep your camp meals simple.

### Suggested Dinners

Macaroni & Cheese (add dried soup, canned or dehydrated meat)

Noodle dinners (including Ramen)

Potato dishes (mashed potatoes, au gratin, or other packaged potatoes)

Minute Rice topped with instant gravies and sauces

Lentils

Instant mashed potatoes

Pasta salads (in a box)

Couscous

Pilafs (lentil, wheat, rice, etc.)

Tuna and other cannned meats

Pepperoni, dried meats, sausages

Sardines and fish steaks

Specialty dehydrated meals

Dehydrated vegetables

# Dinner Recipes

### Curried Rice & Tuna

| | |
|---|---|
| 2 cups instant rice | 4 cups water |
| 1/2 teaspoon salt | 2 teaspoons margarine |
| 1/2 cup seedless raisins | 2 teaspoons curry powder |
| 1 6-ounce can tuna in water | 1 hardboiled egg |

Cook the rice according to the package directions, using the water, salt, and margarine from the ingredients listed above. While rice is cooking, peal the hard-boiled egg and finely chop. Drain most of the water from the tuna (away from the camp). When the rice is cooked, leave over low flame and toss the raisins, curry, chopped boiled eggs, and tuna with a small amount of tuna water. Mix thoroughly and heat briefly. Remove from heat and serve. A couple of tablespoons of chopped almonds makes a good addition to this recipe.

### Tuna Spaghetti

| | |
|---|---|
| 1 8-ounce package angel hair pasta | 1 6-ounce can tuna in oil |
| 8 sun dried tomatoes, sliced | 1 teaspoon dried basil |
| 1 teaspoon oregano | 1/4 cup parmesan cheese |
| 1/2 teaspoon garlic powder | 4 cups water |

*At home:* Mix the basil, oregano, parmesan cheese and garlic powder in a resealable plastic bag and label.

*In camp:* Soak sun dried tomatoes in four cups of water for ten minutes. Remove the tomatoes from water and bring to a boil. Break the angel hair pasta in half and add to the boiling water. Cook pasta until done, usually four or five minutes, depending on how firm you like it. Drain water away from camp. Leave noodles in the pot and add tuna with oil, tomatoes, and contents of the cheese and spice package you assembled at home. Stir well.

A low fat version can be made with water-packed tuna, but you'll want to drain most of the water before adding. If weight is not a factor, two small cans of tomato purée can be used in place of the sun dried tomatoes. This meal goes good with bread fried in margarine and garlic.

**Oyster-stuffed Potatoes**

2 large baking potatoes                    2 cans smoked oysters
4 shitake mushrooms

*At home:* Bake potatoes.

*In Camp:* Rehydrate shitake mushrooms by covering with water and soaking
for 15 minutes. Drain oysters and the mushroom water well away from camp.
Cut open the potatoes and stuff with oysters and mushrooms.

**Chicken Quesadillas**

4-5 small flour or corn tortillas          1 6-ounce can chicken
1 small onion                              1 teaspoon oil
4 ounces monterey jack (with jalepeno peppers if you like it spicy)

Dice onion, packing out the outer skin and end pieces. Thinly slice up cheese.
Drain the chicken well away from camp. Assemble quesadillas by sprinkling
chicken, onion, and cheese on half of the tortilla. Fold the tortilla over omelet-
style and lightly brown in oil.

**Chicken Stroganoff**

1 8-ounce package noodles                  1 6-ounce can chicken
1 packet onion soup mix                    1 small can sliced mushrooms
4 tablespoons sour cream
  (made from dry mix)

Bring water to a boil; add onion soup mix and stir until dissolved. Add noodles
with the soup and cook until tender, 8-10 minutes. Drain water well away from
camp, keeping as much of the onion as possible. Add sour cream, mushrooms,
and chicken. Season to taste. This recipe also works with canned ham or
Textured Vegetable Protein (see the vegetarian section for more on TVP).

## Corned Beef and Potatoes

1 package au gratin potatoes
1 large carrot
2 tablespoon margarine

1 canned corned beef
1 small onion
1/3 cup non-fat dry milk

*At home:* Open potatoes and remove the cheese sauce. Mix the cheese sauce powder with the dry milk in a resealable plastic bag. Leave the potatoes in original package.

*In camp:* Slice carrot into thin, round pieces while bringing the water to a boil. Put dried potatoes and carrot slices into the boiling water and cook until potatoes are tender. While potatoes are cooking, dice onion. When the potatoes are done, drain the water well away from camp, leaving about 1/3 cup of water in the pot with the potatoes and carrots. Add dry milk/cheese sauce mixture and diced onion; stir well. Cut corned beef into pieces as you add it to the pot. Return to heat, stirring continuously until the beef is heated and everything is well mixed.

## Ham a la Ramen

1-2 packages Ramen (oriental noodle soup)
1/2 cup dried peas
Parmesan cheese to taste

1 5 ounce can ham
Red pepper flakes to taste

Cook the Ramen noodles (without the flavor pack) along with the dried peas. When the noodles are cooked, drain away from camp. Top with ham and add red pepper and parmesan cheese to taste. Mix, eat and enjoy.

## Pizza on a Pita

3 whole wheat pitas
4 ounces of mozarella cheese
1 teaspoon of vegetable oil

1 small jar or can of pizza sauce
Pepperoni or other toppings

Cut pitas in half by separating at the edges to make two pizza crusts out of each pita. Top pita halves with pizza sauce, cheese and toppings. Fry in oil until crust is lightly browned.

# Vegetarian Food

Many backpacking meals, such as macaroni and cheese, can be made meatless. But most vegetarians are accustomed to more variety than that in their meals. Several vegetarian favorites work as well on the trail as they do at home. Your backcountry menu can include Textured Vegetable Protein (TVP) and tofu as well as quinoa, lentils, and bulgur wheat.

TVP comes in several flavors and textures, including granules, chunks, and simulated sliced steak. Consisting of soybeans and wheat gluten, it has almost no fat and cholesterol and abounds in vitamins and minerals, protein, and all eight essential amino acids. As an added bonus, TVP is lightweight, won't spoil, is easily rehydrated, and is filling.

Quinoa (pronounced keen-wah) is another excellent hiker food. This grain, originally from South America, is loaded with protein. It's only drawback is that it must be cooked for 20 minutes. No problem! You can always cook it at home and carry it with you in a sealed plastic bag. Quinoa is not available in many grocery stores and is usually purchased from health food stores.

## Vegetarian recipes

### Quick and Easy Soup
1 package instant vegetable soup (Knorr or Lipton—8 servings)
1 cup TVP chunks or granules          Cheddar or other cheese
8 ounces wide egg noodles             Spices to taste

*At home:* Combine the soup mix and spices in a resealable plastic bag, label "Quick and Easy Soup," and include directions. Make sure TVP is in a resealable bag as well because it will expand when wet.

*At camp:* Reconstitute TVP by mixing with one cup boiling water and allowing it to sit for 5-10 minutes. Once TVP is reconstituted, make soup according to directions, adding about 20 percent more water. Add soup mix with spices and TVP to the cold water. When boiling, add noodles and simmer for about five minutes. Add thinly sliced cheese to soup just before serving.

## Tofu Chili

| | |
|---|---|
| 16 ounces tofu | 1 onion or dried onion flakes |
| 1 summer squash (optional) | 1 green pepper (optional) |
| 2 tablespoons oil | 3 tablespoons chili powder |
| 2 cans stewed tomatoes or | 1 can kidney beans or dehydrated beans |
| comparable amount | 1 can black beans or dehydrated beans |
| powdered tomato sauce | |

If using dried beans, rehydrate before cooking. You can do this at home, packing the beans in a resealable bag.

Chop vegetables and tofu. Sauté the onions and green pepper. Stir in chili powder and cook for a minute before adding tomatoes, beans, squash, tofu, and two cups water. Heat to boiling then simmer uncovered 15 minutes or so. If you like, add shredded cheddar to the top. Serves 6.

## Cuban Quinoa

| | |
|---|---|
| 1 cup Quinoa | Vegetable broth |
| 1 can black beans or | 1 onion or dried onion flakes |
| comparable amount dry | 1 tablespoon oil |
| 2-3 garlic cloves or garlic granules | 1 green pepper (optional) |
| or powder beans | |

*At home:* It takes 20 minutes or more to prepare quinoa, so you may want to cook it at home and bring it along in a resealable bag. Cook quinoa in vegetable broth.

*In camp:* If any ingredients need rehydrating, do that first. Sauté onion, garlic, and green pepper in oil; add beans and cook until tender. Serve over quinoa. For added spice, carry along a small jar of salsa. Serves 2 to 3.

**Middle Eastern Stew**

| | |
|---|---|
| 1 cup couscous | Vegetable broth |
| 1 eggplant,diced | 2 tablespoons olive oil |
| 2-3 garlic cloves | Feta cheese |
| 2 zucchini or 1 each zucchini | 8 oz can tomatoes |
| and summer squash, diced | or 8 sun-dried tomatoes |

If using sun-dried tomatoes, rehydrate in four cups hot water for 10 minutes or until soft. Sauté vegetables and garlic in olive oil; cover and simmer until done. Meanwhile bring two cups water and vegetable broth to boil, add couscous and remove from heat. Wait five minutes allowing couscous to absorb all the water. Serve vegetables over couscous and sprinkle with feta cheese.

# Backcountry Baking

Many hikers swear by backcountry baking. And when you think about it, wouldn't you rather eat freshly baked cinnamon rolls for breakfast than rehydrated scrambled eggs? How about cheese bread to go with your spaghetti and smoked sausage for dinner?

**Wouldn't you rather eat freshly baked cinnamon rolls for breakfast.**

There are a number of "ovens" made specifically for backcountry baking; two of the most popular are the Bakepacker and the Outback Oven. The Bakepacker, produced by Strike 2 Industries, Inc., can be used for baking or just about anything else. Similarly, the Outback Oven bakes as well as boils, frys, etc.

Both the Bakepacker and Outback Oven come in two sizes; the ultralights fit most backpacking cook sets and uses your own cook pot for baking. The larger Bakepacker also uses your personal cookset but is usually too big for most backpacking cook sets. On the other hand, the Outback Oven Plus Ten comes with its own teflon baking pan and lid with a thermometer on the knob.

# Baking Recipes

### Starter Dough

2 cups lukewarm water
1 teaspoon salt (optional)
2 tablespoons sugar, brown sugar,
  molasses, or honey

1 tablespoon yeast
1-2 tablespoons oil (optional)
4-5 cups flour

Combine first five ingredients in a warm, preferably insulated, bowl or cup. When mixture begins to bubble, combine with two cups of flour (wheat, white or both). Mix with a spoon for three to four minutes until dough is stringy. Continue to add flour slowly, kneading until dough becomes an unsticky ball that holds its shape. Place dough in well-oiled pot and setting it in the sun to rise. If it is not sunny, grease the dough, put it in a plastic bag, and place it somewhere warm to rise—inside your clothes or in the bottom of a sleeping bag near your feet. Or, if you don't want to mix up the dough in the morning, make it at night, double bag it and sleep with it. The dough doesn't have to rise, but the more it rises the lighter it becomes. Before baking, knead the dough for a few minutes.

### Cinnamon Rolls

Starter dough
Sugar
Raisins (optional)

Butter
Cinnamon
Nuts (optional)

After kneading your starter dough for the second time as described above, roll the dough out into a thin sheet. Spread with butter, sugar, and cinnamon. Add raisins and nuts if you wish. Roll into a log and pinch the ends shut. Spiral the log into a well-oiled baking pan and spread more butter on top.

*To bake:* Use a Bakepacker or Outback Oven and follow directions for baking or you can use a Dutch oven or frying pan with a tight-fitting lid. After gathering a pile of pencil-thick sticks, light your stove, and run it at its lowest heat. Put your baking pan on the stove and use the twigs to build a fire on its lid. Spread the fire as evenly as possible and continue to feed it twigs to keep it burning. Rotate the pan every five minutes or so to assure even cooking. The bread should take 30 to 45 minutes, but check it sooner if the aroma of baking bread is particularly strong. You'll know it is done when the bread has a firm crust and sounds hollow when thumped. When done, remove from the stove, but let the twig fire burn down completely before removing the bread.

## Cheese Bread
Starter dough                                  Cheese of choice
Herbs and spices to taste

This variation on the cinnamon rolls above is a better alternative for dinner. As in the recipe above, roll out the dough and layer with cheese and spices before rolling up. Bake as directed above.

## Pizza
Starter dough              Pizza sauce (brought from home or made in camp)
Cheese                     Pepperoni or whatever you like on a pizza

This recipe will make two pizzas if you wish. Otherwise, use only half the starter dough or cut the recipe in half. After kneading a second time, press the dough into a well-oiled baking pan. Top with sauce and your choice of ingredients. Bake for 20 to 30 minutes, following the directions above.

    If you like crispy crust, it is not necessary for the dough to rise.

# Snacks

Between-meal snacks are an important way to keep up your energy level while hiking. Some hikers swear by candy bars and other store-bought snacks. Gorp, a longtime favorite, is always a popular choice for an easy burst of calories at a rest break.

### G.O.R.P. Recipe

"Good Old Raisins and Peanuts" is not *a* backpacking snack, it is *the* backpacking snack. The mystical blend makes an easy to make, easy to eat snack that is nutritious to boot. The following is a list of ingredients often found in gorp, but you can make up your own combinations.

Peanuts or other nuts
Raisins (plain, chocolate or yogurt covered)
M & Ms
Cheerios or other cereal
Chopped dried fruit
Shredded coconut
Reese's Pieces
Sunflower seeds

# Beverages

Keeping your body hydrated is one of the most important aspects of healthy backpacking, and water is the best choice for doing this. But there will be times when your treated water (boiled or iodined) will taste terrible and you'll probably want to disguise the flavor. The best powdered drink mix to use is an electrolyte solution such as Gatorade or Gookinaid ERG. These will replace the electrolytes and fluids you lose when you perspire.

Caffeine has a diuretic effect on the body; so if you consume drinks that contain caffeine, keep in mind that you will need to drink extra water when hiking. Or consider switching to decaf.

**Suggested Beverages**
Water
Fruit drink mix (Kool-Aid, Crystal Light, etc.)
Iced tea or fruit tea mix
Jello mix (a tasty, hot drink that also supplies extra calories)
Tea (herbal, etc. in bags)
Instant coffee
Spiced cider mix
Powdered egg nog
Electrolyte drink mix
Cocoa/hot chocolate
Non-dairy creamer (for tea/coffee)

**Camp-brewed Coffee**
Can't stand the thought of instant coffee? You can always brew your own over a cook stove or campfire. Here are two different methods:

Bring a measured amount of cold water to a rolling boil in a coffee pot or your cooking pot. Remove from the stove or campfire, add the coffee, and let it steep for ten minutes. Make sure the pot is tightly covered and in a warm place. You will want to strain the coffee as you pour it into your mug.

Another way to make coffee is to add the cold water and coffee together and then bring the water to a boil. As soon as it boils, take the pot off the heat and let the liquid steep for five minutes. Once again, make sure the pot is tightly capped and in a warm place.

Never boil coffee for any length of time as boiling can make it very bitter. If you don't want to grind coffee beans in the outdoors (by pounding them against a rock while wrapped in a cloth, of course) grind them before leaving home. Obviously, the fresher the coffee, the better the taste.

# Dessert

Still hungry? Top off your camp meal with an instant pudding or cheesecake mix. Before you leave home, add powdered milk and a teaspoon of non-dairy creamer to the dry mix. To prepare in camp, add water slowly while stirring; generally it is better to use a little less water or milk than the directions call for.

Don't forget s'mores, the favorite recipe of many a Girl Scout troop. Toast a marshmallow or two over a fire and then form a sandwich using the the hot marshmallow in between two pieces of graham cracker with a slab of chocolate bar. The heat from the marshmallow melts the chocolate and the result is delicious.

# Dessert Recipes

### Baked Apples
2 apples                    2 teaspoons margarine
2 pinches cinnamon

Core apples and fill each with a teaspoon of margarine and a pinch of cinnamon. Wrap tightly in a double layer of aluminum foil. Drop in the coals of a fire that you've let die down a little; cover with other coals. After 10 minutes, fish out the foil wrapped apples, carefully unwrap, and enjoy.

### Stuffed Bananas
Two bananas                 2 teaspoons mint or plain chocolate chips

Leave the peel on the bananas and cut a slit deep down the side of each. Stuff a teaspoon of chips into each banana and wrap in a double layer of aluminum foil. Cover in coals and bake for 10 minutes. Eat with a spoon. Nuts and marshmallows also make for great stuffed bananas.

# Spices

Camp food can be improved with a few lightweight spices that you can squirrel away in your pack. Many hikers use the plastic containers from 35mm film, but Kodak highly discourages this. Chemicals present in the container can leach into the spices and food, posing a health risk. Special containers are available at outdoors stores.

**Suggested Spices**
(You may have your own favorites:)
Garlic
Salt
Pepper
Italian seasoning
Seasoned "butter"
Tabasco or other hot sauce
Red pepper
Curry powder
Chili powder
Oregano
Cumin
Onion powder

# Cleaning Up After Meals

You've finished eating one of your one-pot miracles hot off the stove, and it's time to kick back and enjoy the view, read a book, or write in a journal. Not quite yet. The best time to clean up is immediately after a meal. Not only will that keep ants and other bugs from seeking out your leftovers, but your dishes will clean up easier right away.

**The best time to clean up is immediately after a meal.**

When getting your cooking water, always bring extra water for cleaning up after meals. Never wash your dishes directly in a stream. You should be at least 100 yards away from any water source when you wash the dishes so that your fellow campers don't get the dubious benefits of your dirty dish water. Any leftover food scraps go in the bag with trash that you are packing out. Dumping it near the campsite isn't just unsightly; even buried food scraps can attract raccoons and other animals. Once tempted, the scavengers will go through everything looking for more food.

Wash the dishes and utensils in warm water with biodegradable soap. Clean the pots, dishes and utensils with a scrubber. Many hikers use steel wool, but we prefer a non-abrasive scrub pad. When finished, scatter the wash water over a wide area, well away from both the water source and the campsite. Rinse with water and scatter again.

**Giardia can still be found hanging on to your pots after they have dried.**

Giardia can still be found hanging on to your pots after they have been thoroughly washed and dried, so boil some water and in the pot for a final purified rinse. If you have a water filter, you can do the last rinse with filtered water, saving on fuel for your stove.

# Packing Food for the Backcountry

You've read through the book and selected a menu. Now it's time to pack your food. As noted in our recipes, you will want to open the boxes that pasta and other packaged supermarket foods come in. All of the spices used together in a meal can be packed together in one small resealable plastic bag. If you are making the Ham a la Ramen, for example, you would take the oriental noodles out of their package and pack them together with a measured amount of dried peas in a plastic bag. Drop the directions in the bag with them and seal it up.

If several meals will require powdered milk, you may want to bring it along in a separate bag. For a creamier taste, add a teaspoon of non-dairy creamer in for each cup of dry milk. Be sure to double bag the dry milk, as even a pinhole can cause a mess inside your pack.

Oil for your recipes can be carried in a small glass or plastic jar. As we mentioned earlier, don't use a plastic 35mm film container as harmful chemicals can leach out into the oil. You will want to keep your oil container in a resealable plastic bag so that a small leak won't make a big mess.

By now you are probably picturing the inside of your pack stuffed with plastic bags and wondering if this is all that good for the environment. Perhaps not, so you will want to reuse them for a number of trips. After carrying pasta on one hike, a bag should still be in great shape to reuse several times. If they do get dirty, they can easily be washed out at home. However, never reuse a bag that has carried uncooked meat.

# Storing Food for the Night

Food, soap, and other smellables often prove too much temptation for mice, raccoons, bears, and other campsite scavengers. Put all your smellables together in a bag. Some campgrounds frequented by persistent pests have boxes or cages for storing food at night. If not, you will have to hang your smellables from a tree. Secure a rope over a tree limb, tie the bag to the rope, pull it up, and tie it off for the night. The bag should be ten feet off the ground and ten feet from the nearest tree if possible. If rain is expected, use a big trash bag to hold the food.